Navigating Life

7 Essential Lessons Learned Onboard a Cruise Ship

by Tiffany Budert-Waltz

Dedication

To my fiancé, Abdullah, who took me on my first cruise and inspired me to write this book.

Acknowledgments

I would like to express my deepest gratitude to all those who have supported me.

Table of Contents

Preface

Introduction: Embarking on the Voyage

Chapter 1: Riding the Waves of Uncertainty	1
Chapter 2: Acts of Kindness in Open Waters	6
Chapter 3: Conversations at Sea	10
Chapter 4: Stories from the Deck	14
Chapter 5: Navigating Change with Grace	18
Chapter 6: Finding Still Waters	22
Chapter 7: Gratitude from Port to Port	25
Conclusion: Beyond the Horizon	29
Author Bio	31

Preface

I have always been fascinated by the sea and the stories it holds. The vastness and mystery of the ocean have always captivated my imagination, inspiring dreams of adventures and discoveries. This book is a culmination of my lifelong love for the ocean and my passion for exploring the deeper currents of human experience.

"Navigating Life" was born from a desire to share the profound lessons I have learned through my journeys, both literal and metaphorical. Life, much like a voyage at sea, is filled with unpredictable challenges and unexpected joys. Through this book, I hope to offer readers a compass to navigate their own journeys with greater resilience, empathy, and understanding.

This book is organized into seven chapters, each focusing on a specific life lesson gleaned from my experiences on a cruise ship. Each chapter weaves together personal anecdotes, emotional insights, and practical advice to illuminate a guiding principle for navigating life's complexities. From embracing uncertainty to cultivating gratitude, these lessons are universal and timeless.

The journey that inspired this book was not just a physical voyage but a transformative experience that reshaped my perspective on life. As you embark on this journey with me, I invite you to reflect on your own experiences, find resonance in the stories shared, and discover your own guiding principles.

Introduction: Embarking on the Voyage

The cruise began with a sense of excitement and anticipation. The passengers boarded the majestic ship, their faces glowing with the promise of adventure and relaxation as they departed from the vibrant port of Miami. The sun shone brightly, reflecting off the sleek vessel as it embarked on its journey across the sparkling blue waters. The itinerary was meticulously planned, with stops at picturesque Caribbean islands and bustling ports. However, nature had its own plans.

As I stood on the deck, feeling the warm sea breeze and watching the coastline fade into the horizon, I couldn't help but feel a mix of emotions. There was a thrill in the unknown, a curiosity about the adventures that awaited. Little did I know that this journey would not only take me to beautiful destinations but also lead me to profound insights about life and the human experience.

Throughout the voyage, I encountered moments of joy, surprise, and reflection. The sea, with its ever-changing moods and vastness, became a powerful metaphor for life itself. Each day brought new experiences, challenges, and opportunities for growth. From the camaraderie of fellow passengers to the quiet moments of solitude, every aspect of the cruise offered valuable lessons that I carried with me long after the journey ended.

This book is a reflection of those lessons, distilled into seven essential principles that can help navigate the complexities of life. Whether you are facing uncertainty, seeking deeper connections, or looking for ways to cultivate gratitude, these lessons are designed to provide guidance and inspiration.

As you embark on this voyage with me, I invite you to immerse yourself in the stories and reflections shared within these pages. Let the sea be your guide, and may these lessons illuminate your path, helping you navigate life's challenges with resilience and grace.

Chapter 1: Riding the Waves of Uncertainty

The cruise began with a sense of excitement and anticipation. The passengers boarded the majestic ship, their faces glowing with the promise of adventure and relaxation as they departed from the vibrant port of Miami. The sun shone brightly, reflecting off the sleek vessel as it embarked on its journey across the sparkling blue waters. The itinerary was meticulously planned, with stops at picturesque Caribbean islands and bustling ports. However, nature had its own plans.

On the second day at sea, the sky darkened unexpectedly. What started as a mild drizzle quickly escalated into a fierce storm. The captain announced that due to the severe weather conditions, the planned stop at the first port had to be canceled. Instead, the ship would take a longer route, avoiding the storm's path. The atmosphere on the ship shifted dramatically. Murmurs of disappointment and frustration filled the air as passengers grappled with the change in plans.

The storm served as a powerful metaphor for life's unpredictability. Just as the passengers had to adjust their expectations and plans, life often throws unexpected challenges our way. How we respond to these uncertainties can shape our growth and open doors to new opportunities.

The initial reaction to the change in itinerary was a mix of anxiety and frustration. Many passengers felt their dream vacation was being ruined. It's natural to feel disoriented and upset when plans go awry. Recognizing and accepting these emotions is the first step towards managing them effectively.

Anxiety: The unknown can be daunting. The fear of what might happen, the discomfort of changing plans, and the loss of control contribute to anxiety.
Frustration: When things don't go as planned, it's easy to feel frustrated and disappointed.

Developing emotional intelligence involves acknowledging our feelings and finding constructive ways to cope with them. Here are some techniques for managing emotions during uncertain times:

1. Mindfulness: Practice being present in the moment. Mindfulness helps in grounding oneself and reducing anxiety.
2. Positive Reframing: Instead of focusing on what's lost, look for what can be gained. This shift in perspective can transform frustration into curiosity and excitement.
3. Deep Breathing: Simple deep breathing exercises can calm the mind and body, helping to manage stress.

As the storm raged outside, I decided to explore the ship and observe how others were coping. I noticed a group of passengers gathered in the lounge, engaged in a lively conversation. Their laughter and camaraderie were infectious. Some decided to make the most of the situation by heading to the karaoke bar, where they sang their favorite songs, creating a joyful and carefree atmosphere. Others chose to visit the casino, trying their luck at various games and embracing the thrill of chance. These impromptu activities highlighted the diverse ways people cope with uncertainty – through joyous expression or calculated risk-taking.

Karaoke: This spontaneous activity fostered a sense of community and provided an emotional release. Singing and laughing together helped to alleviate stress and build connections among passengers.

Casino: Engaging in casino games offered a different form of distraction, focusing on strategy and luck. This activity allowed passengers to channel their uncertainty into controlled environments, providing both excitement and a sense of agency.

Reflecting on this experience, I recalled other moments in my life where uncertainty led to significant personal growth. One such instance was when I decided to move to a new city where I knew no one. Initially, the fear and uncertainty were overwhelming. However, this decision pushed me to step out of my comfort zone, make new connections, and ultimately discover a new side of myself.

Broader Implications: Embracing uncertainty is not just about accepting what we cannot change, but also about actively seeking the silver lining in every situation. This mindset shift can lead to new opportunities and personal growth.

Another example from my life was during a solo trip to a foreign country. Language barriers and unfamiliar surroundings initially made me anxious. However, by embracing the uncertainty and stepping out of my comfort zone, I ended up having some of the most enriching experiences, meeting incredible people, and gaining a deeper understanding of different cultures.

The storm on the cruise was a reminder that life is full of unexpected twists and turns. While it's natural to feel anxious and frustrated, developing emotional intelligence can help us navigate these challenges with grace and resilience. By embracing uncertainty, we open ourselves up to new opportunities and personal growth.

Chapter 2: Acts of Kindness in Open Waters

The cruise ship glided smoothly through the calm waters, leaving the stormy weather behind. The sun re-emerged, casting a golden glow over the expansive ocean. Passengers slowly returned to their routines, exploring the ship's numerous amenities and enjoying the newfound serenity. Amidst this backdrop of tranquility, acts of kindness began to surface, weaving a sense of community among the passengers.

One morning, while enjoying breakfast at the ship's buffet, I noticed an elderly woman struggling to carry her tray. Without hesitation, a young man nearby stepped in to help her, offering a warm smile as he guided her to a table. Later that day, as I strolled along the deck, I saw a group of strangers mingling and sharing sunscreen with each other, their laughter echoing through the air. These small yet significant gestures of kindness created a ripple effect, fostering a sense of camaraderie among the passengers.

These acts of kindness, though seemingly minor, had a profound impact on the atmosphere aboard the ship. They served as a reminder that kindness costs nothing but has immense value in enriching our lives and the lives of others. Small gestures can transform ordinary moments into meaningful connections, making a significant difference in the overall experience.

Recognizing the emotions associated with acts of kindness helps us understand their importance and impact.

Empathy: Feeling empathy when witnessing or engaging in acts of kindness.
Compassion: Understanding the joy and fulfillment that come from helping others.
Gratitude: Experiencing gratitude when receiving kindness from others.

Practicing and appreciating acts of kindness can enhance our emotional intelligence. Here are some ways to cultivate and recognize kindness in our daily lives:

1. Mindful Awareness: Pay attention to opportunities for kindness in everyday interactions.

2. Expressing Gratitude: Show appreciation for acts of kindness received, reinforcing positive behavior.

3. Encouraging Empathy: Actively put yourself in others' shoes to understand their needs and feelings.

During the cruise, I observed many more examples of kindness. One evening, I joined a painting session where passengers were invited to contribute to a large mural depicting the journey of the ship. This collaborative art project brought people together, each person adding their unique touch to the mural. The act of painting together fostered a sense of unity and shared purpose, with everyone working towards a common goal.

Reflecting on these moments, I remembered a time when a simple act of kindness had a lasting impact on me. During a particularly challenging period at work, a colleague offered to help me with my workload without expecting anything in return. This gesture not only alleviated my stress but also strengthened our professional relationship and created a positive working environment.

Broader Implications: Acts of kindness, no matter how small, have the power to create a ripple effect that extends beyond the immediate moment. They can build stronger communities, foster positive relationships, and contribute to a more compassionate world.

Another example from my life was when I volunteered as a track coach. The simple act of offering my time and skills to help those who needed guidance brought immense fulfillment and a sense of connection to my community. It reminded me that kindness is a powerful force that can make a significant difference in the lives of others.

The acts of kindness observed during the cruise highlighted the importance of empathy and compassion in our interactions. By practicing and appreciating kindness, we can enhance our emotional intelligence, build deeper connections, and create a more positive and supportive environment for ourselves and others.

Chapter 3: Conversations at Sea

Conversations at sea take on a unique depth and quality, influenced by the tranquility of the ocean and the absence of everyday distractions. As the cruise progressed, I found myself engaging in meaningful dialogues with fellow passengers. These conversations, often sparked by the shared experience of the journey, led to profound insights and connections.

One evening, I joined a group of travelers in the ship's lounge. As the gentle sway of the ship rocked us back and forth, we shared stories of our lives, our dreams, and our challenges. The environment encouraged openness and vulnerability, allowing us to connect on a deeper level. I spoke with a retired teacher who shared her passion for education and the impact she had on her students' lives. Her stories were inspiring and reminded me of the importance of pursuing one's passions.

These conversations highlighted the importance of active listening and empathy. By truly listening to others, we can gain new perspectives and build stronger relationships.

Recognizing the emotions associated with deep conversations helps us appreciate their value.

Empathy: Feeling a deep connection and understanding of others' experiences.
Curiosity: A genuine interest in learning about others and their stories.
Fulfillment: The joy and satisfaction derived from meaningful interactions.

Engaging in deep conversations can enhance our emotional intelligence. Here are some ways to foster and benefit from such interactions:

1. Active Listening: Focus on the speaker, avoid interrupting, and show genuine interest in their words.
2. Open-Ended Questions: Ask questions that encourage detailed responses and deeper insights.
3. Empathetic Responses: Validate the speaker's feelings and experiences, showing that you understand and care.

Reflecting on these conversations, I recalled a time when a deep conversation had a significant impact on my life. During a challenging period, a friend took the time to listen to my concerns and offer support. This interaction not only provided comfort but also strengthened our friendship and helped me gain clarity on my situation.

Broader Implications: Deep conversations can lead to personal growth, strengthened relationships, and a greater understanding of others. By actively listening and engaging with empathy, we can build more meaningful connections.

Another example from my life was when I participated in a community dialogue event. The event brought together people from diverse backgrounds to discuss important social issues. Through these conversations, I gained new perspectives and developed a deeper appreciation for the experiences and viewpoints of others. It reinforced the idea that meaningful dialogue can bridge divides and foster understanding.

The conversations at sea underscored the value of meaningful interactions and the importance of active listening. By engaging in deep conversations, we can enhance our emotional intelligence, build stronger relationships, and gain valuable insights into ourselves and others.

Chapter 4: Stories from the Deck

The deck of the cruise ship became a place where stories were shared and memories were made. As we sailed through calm waters and under starlit skies, passengers gathered on the deck to share their stories, each one adding to the rich tapestry of the journey.

One afternoon, I sat with a group of passengers who were exchanging travel tales. There was a couple who had visited over fifty countries, each with its unique adventures and lessons. Their stories were filled with excitement, humor, and moments of awe. Listening to them, I felt a deep appreciation for the diverse experiences that life offers.

These storytelling sessions highlighted the power of narratives in connecting us to each other and to our own experiences. Stories have the ability to transport us, evoke emotions, and provide insights into different cultures and perspectives.

Recognizing the emotions associated with storytelling helps us understand its impact.

Connection: Feeling a sense of belonging and shared experience.
Inspiration: Being motivated and uplifted by others' stories.
Reflection: Gaining insights and understanding through shared narratives.

Engaging in storytelling can enhance our emotional intelligence. Here are some ways to appreciate and benefit from storytelling:

1. Active Participation: Engage with the storyteller, showing interest and asking questions.
2. Sharing Your Own Stories: Be open to sharing your experiences, fostering mutual connection.
3. Reflecting on Stories: Take time to reflect on the stories you hear and the emotions they evoke.

Reflecting on these storytelling sessions, I remembered a

time when sharing my story had a profound impact on me. During a community event, I shared my journey of overcoming a personal challenge. The act of sharing not only helped me process my experiences but also connected me with others who had faced similar struggles. It was a powerful reminder of the healing and connecting power of stories.

Broader Implications: Storytelling is a fundamental human experience that fosters connection, understanding, and personal growth. By sharing and listening to stories, we can build deeper relationships and gain new perspectives.

Another example from my life was during a family reunion. As we gathered around the dinner table, my relatives shared stories of our family's history, recounting tales of resilience, love, and adventure. These stories not only strengthened our family bonds but also instilled a sense of pride and continuity.

The stories shared on the deck of the cruise ship underscored the importance of narratives in our lives. By engaging in storytelling, we can enhance our emotional intelligence, connect with others on a deeper level, and find inspiration and reflection in shared experiences.

Chapter 5: Navigating Change with Grace

Change is an inevitable part of life, and the ability to navigate it with grace is a valuable skill. The cruise provided numerous opportunities to witness and practice this skill, as plans changed and new experiences unfolded.

One day, the captain announced that due to unforeseen circumstances, our itinerary would be altered. Instead of visiting a bustling port city, we would spend an extra day at sea. While some passengers were disappointed, others saw this as an opportunity to relax and enjoy the ship's amenities. I decided to make the most of the situation by exploring parts of the ship I hadn't yet visited and engaging in activities I had initially overlooked.

This change in plans reminded me of the importance of flexibility and adaptability. Life often requires us to adjust our expectations and embrace new opportunities, even when they are unexpected.

Recognizing the emotions associated with change helps us manage our responses.

Adaptability: The ability to adjust to new situations with a positive outlook.
Resilience: The strength to recover from setbacks and continue moving forward.
Open-Mindedness: Being open to new experiences and perspectives.

Developing emotional intelligence involves cultivating these traits. Here are some ways to navigate change with grace:

1. Embracing Flexibility: Be willing to adjust your plans and expectations as needed.
2. Finding Silver Linings: Look for the positive aspects of new situations and opportunities for growth.
3. Practicing Resilience: Build resilience by focusing on your strengths and learning from challenges.

Reflecting on this experience, I recalled a time when

navigating change with grace had a significant impact on my life. During my college years, I faced an unexpected challenge when I had to change my major. Initially, the idea of switching from a field I was comfortable with to something entirely new was daunting. However, by remaining flexible and open-minded, I discovered a passion for my new field of study. This change not only broadened my horizons but also opened up new opportunities for growth and development.

Broader Implications: Navigating change with grace can lead to personal and professional growth. By embracing flexibility, resilience, and open-mindedness, we can turn challenges into opportunities.

Another example from my life was when I decided to pursue a new career path. The transition was filled with uncertainties and challenges, but by staying adaptable and resilient, I was able to find success and fulfillment in my new field.

The experiences on the cruise underscored the importance of navigating change with grace. By developing emotional intelligence and cultivating adaptability, resilience, and open-mindedness, we can manage life's inevitable changes with confidence and positivity.

Chapter 6: Finding Still Waters

In the midst of a busy and often chaotic world, finding moments of stillness and calm can be incredibly rejuvenating. The cruise provided the perfect setting for such moments, with the vast ocean serving as a backdrop for reflection and relaxation.

One morning, I woke up early to watch the sunrise from the deck. The sky was painted with hues of orange and pink, and the ocean was calm and serene. As I stood there, taking in the beauty of the moment, I felt a deep sense of peace and clarity. It was a reminder of the importance of taking time to pause and reflect amidst the busyness of life.

These moments of stillness are essential for maintaining emotional balance and mental clarity. They provide an opportunity to reconnect with ourselves and gain perspective.

Recognizing the emotions associated with stillness helps us

appreciate its value.

Calm: A sense of tranquility and peace.
Clarity: Mental and emotional clarity that comes from reflection.
Rejuvenation: Feeling refreshed and recharged after moments of stillness.

Incorporating moments of stillness into our daily lives can enhance our emotional intelligence. Here are some ways to find and appreciate stillness:

1. Mindful Breathing: Practice deep breathing exercises to calm the mind and body.
2. Nature Walks: Spend time in nature, allowing yourself to be present in the moment.
3. Meditation: Incorporate meditation into your routine to cultivate a sense of inner peace.

Reflecting on these moments of stillness, I remembered a time when finding calm amidst chaos had a profound impact on me. Living in Philadelphia, a city known for its hustle and bustle, I often sought refuge in one of the city's large parks. There, amidst the greenery and tranquility, I would find a quiet spot to write poetry. This practice not only provided mental clarity but also became a cherished routine that allowed me to reconnect with my inner self.

Broader Implications: Finding moments of stillness can significantly enhance our emotional and mental well-being. By incorporating practices that promote calm and reflection, we can navigate life's challenges with greater ease and clarity.

Another example from my life was when I decided to make writing my meditative practice to escape the noise of the city and find peace. By surrounding myself with nature, I could escape the chaos and fully immerse myself in the creative process. These moments of quiet reflection not only helped me gain clarity but also rejuvenated my spirit.

The serene moments on the cruise underscored the value of finding stillness in our lives. By embracing these moments, we can enhance our emotional intelligence, gain clarity, and rejuvenate our spirits.

Chapter 7: Gratitude from Port to Port

As the cruise ship visited different ports, each stop brought new experiences and opportunities for reflection. One of the most powerful lessons I learned during the journey was the importance of cultivating gratitude. Each destination, with its unique charm and beauty, reminded me to appreciate the small and significant moments in life.

During one of the excursions, I visited the Dominican Republic, known for its vibrant culture and friendly locals. As I explored the area, I was struck by the warmth and generosity of the people I met. Their genuine smiles and willingness to share their stories and traditions left a lasting impression on me. It was a reminder to be grateful for the kindness and connections we encounter every day.

Recognizing the emotions associated with gratitude helps us understand its transformative power.

Appreciation: A deep sense of thankfulness for the positive aspects of life.

Contentment: A feeling of satisfaction and happiness with what we have.

Joy: The happiness that comes from recognizing and valuing the good in our lives.

Practicing gratitude can significantly enhance our emotional intelligence. Here are some ways to cultivate and express gratitude:

1. Gratitude Journaling: Keep a journal to regularly write down things you are grateful for.

2. Expressing Thanks: Take the time to thank others for their kindness and support.

3. Mindful Appreciation: Practice mindfulness to fully appreciate and savor the present moment.

Reflecting on the importance of gratitude, I remembered a time when expressing gratitude had a profound impact on my life. After completing a challenging project, I took the time to write thank-you notes to my team members. This simple act of expressing gratitude not only strengthened our professional relationships but also boosted morale and created a positive work environment.

Broader Implications: Cultivating gratitude can lead to increased happiness, improved relationships, and a greater sense of well-being. By appreciating the positive aspects of our lives and expressing gratitude, we can enhance our emotional intelligence and overall satisfaction.

Another example from my life was when I decided to create a gratitude tree in my living room. Each day, I would write down something I was grateful for on a small leaf-shaped note and attach it to the branches of the tree. Over time, the tree blossomed with colorful reminders of positivity and gratitude. This daily practice of mindful appreciation not only helped me focus on the good in my life but also served as a visual reminder of all the things I had to be thankful for.

The various ports of call on the cruise underscored the importance of gratitude. By recognizing and appreciating the positive aspects of our lives, we can cultivate a mindset of gratitude that enhances our emotional intelligence and overall well-being.

Conclusion: Beyond the Horizon

As the cruise journey came to an end, I found myself reflecting on the many lessons learned and the profound impact of the experience. The vastness of the ocean, the tranquility of the still waters, the camaraderie of fellow passengers, and the beauty of each destination had all contributed to a journey of self-discovery and personal growth.

The seven essential lessons learned onboard the cruise ship—embracing uncertainty, practicing kindness, engaging in deep conversations, sharing stories, navigating change with grace, finding stillness, and cultivating gratitude—have illuminated a path for navigating life's complexities with resilience and grace.

As you carry these lessons with you, remember that life, much like a voyage at sea, is filled with unpredictable challenges and unexpected joys. By applying these principles, you can navigate your own journey with greater emotional intelligence and a deeper appreciation for the experiences that shape you.

Thank you for joining me on this journey. May the guiding principles shared in this book illuminate your path, helping you navigate life's challenges with confidence and positivity. As you sail beyond the horizon, may you find joy, fulfillment, and a deeper connection to yourself and the world around you.

Bon voyage!

Author Bio

Tiffany is a passionate writer and avid traveler with a deep love for the sea and the stories it holds. With a background in educational strategy and a commitment to fostering transformative change, Tiffany has dedicated her life to exploring the deeper currents of human experience and sharing insights through storytelling. When not sailing the high seas, Tiffany enjoys mentoring, volunteering, and advocating for social justice and environmental responsibility. "Navigating Life: 7 Essential Lessons Learned Onboard a Cruise Ship" is Tiffany's latest work, inspired by a transformative journey at sea.

Made in the USA
Columbia, SC
29 September 2024